THE
Swan
PRINCE
A Fairy Tale

Starring

Mikhail Baryshnikov

THE
Swan
PRINCE
A Fairy Tale

Conceived by

Mikhail Baryshnikov

WRITTEN AND DIRECTED BY
PETER ANASTOS

PHOTOGRAPHS BY
ARTHUR ELGORT

INTRODUCTION BY
JEAN PONIATOWSKI

BANTAM BOOKS

TORONTO • NEW YORK • LONDON • SYDNEY • AUCKLAND

THE SWAN PRINCE

A Bantam Book / November 1987

Produced by Carol Ford.

All rights reserved.
Copyright © 1987 by Mikhail Baryshnikov, Arthur Elgort, Ltd., and Peter Anastos.
Book design by Barbara N. Cohen.
Layout by Debby Jay.
Photographs copyright © 1987 by Arthur Elgort, Ltd.
This book may not be reproduced in whole or in part, by
mimeograph or any other means, without permission.
For information address: Bantam Books, Inc.

Library of Congress Cataloging-in-Publication Data

Anastos, Peter.
  The swan prince.

  I. Baryshnikov, Mikhail, 1948–   . II. Title.
PS3551.N265S94   1987   811′.54   87-47574
ISBN 0-553-05218-7

Published simultaneously in the United States and Canada

Bantam Books are published by Bantam Books, Inc. Its trademark, consisting of the
words "Bantam Books" and the portrayal of a rooster, is Registered in U.S. Patent and
Trademark Office and in other countries. Marca Registrada. Bantam Books, Inc., 666
Fifth Avenue, New York, New York 10103.

PRINTED IN THE UNITED STATES OF AMERICA

WAK   0 9 8 7 6 5 4 3 2

Once upon a time . . .

It all started when *Paris Vogue* invited Mikhail Baryshnikov to be our guest editor and lead the dance for our Christmas 1986 issue. Among his collaborators, Baryshnikov asked Peter Anastos to join the ballet and write the fairy tale for us. And this is how *The Swan Prince* was born.

Translated into image by photographer Arthur Elgort, Baryshnikov danced the leading role. Through him, The Swan Prince, Siegfried, crosses through the looking glass and becomes real, all for our pleasure.

I am very happy that *Paris Vogue* should have been present at the origin of this poetical *"pas de trois"* and that it contributed in its modest capacity to the fight against AIDS.

Started as "once upon a time . . . ," this book is the happy ending of a Christmas tale.

JEAN PONIATOWSKI
Publisher, *Paris Vogue*

Cast of Characters

PRINCE SIEGFRIED
Mikhail Baryshnikov

THE QUEEN MOTHER
Barbara

DOCTOR TRUDELIESE WEISENHEIMER
Comtesse Helga du Mesnil-Adelée

THE METROPOLITAN NEUROTIKOFF
Charles Engell France

VON ROTHBART
Oscar de la Renta

$\mathcal{O}$nce upon a time there was a Prince named Siegfried. He was sweet, but tragic. You see, *mes enfants*, our Prince had a tragic, but sweet, obsession with swans. Oh, yes, much like his ancestor, the Bavarian Ludwig, he simply adored little feathered creatures . . . swans, that is.

He wasn't remotely interested in anything a proper young member of royalty should be. Oh, no. Not fast cars, or yachts, or gambling, or girls. Not horse racing—or charity, either. Just swans.

Prince Siegfried awoke each morning surrounded by his little feathered friends. No one, not even the most luscious and curvaceous creature in the realm, could come between Siggy and Cygnes. Who can explain it?

He simply preferred birds to chicks.

In the morning, the Prince loved reading stories to his swans . . . wonderful tales about worms and insects, little crumbs and baguettes . . . all the things they adored.

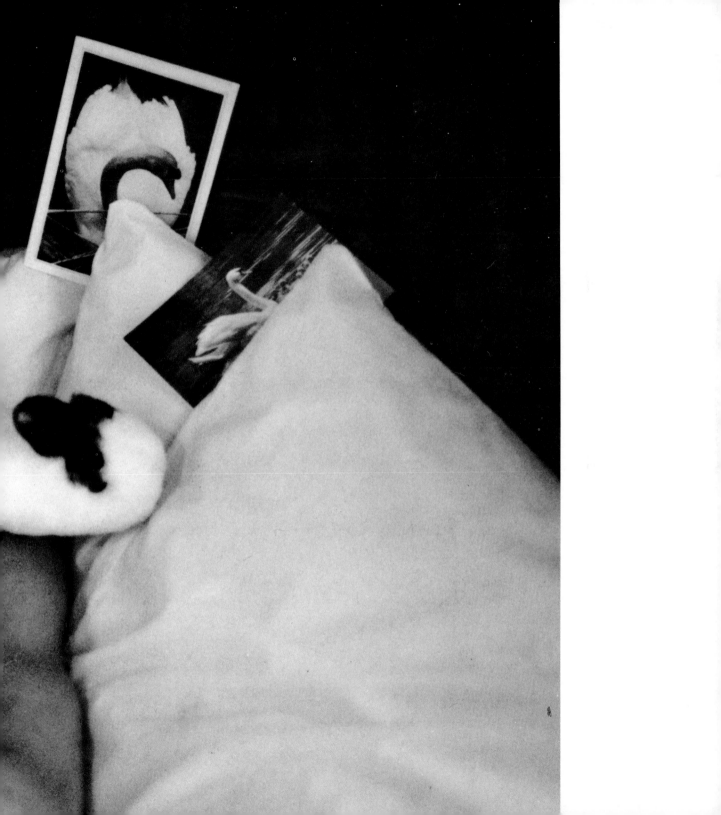

But Siegfried's mother, the Queen, was deeply disturbed by her son's strange behavior.

She had surrounded him with ravishing beauties, delicious damsels, precious princesses, but to no avail. The Prince would not think of marriage.

"How ow will he ever produce an heir?" she lamented.

The Queen summoned the Prince . . .

. . . but he paused for a moment to admire one of his favorite paintings . . .

. . . a John Singer Swansdown.

"You must give up these birds!" she commanded. "Nothing good can come of this relationship." Then she thought for a moment. "Except maybe some pâté."

The Prince shuddered!

The Queen lectured him on proper princely manners.
"You must take up Causes," she instructed him. "Bridge openings, ship christenings, cutting ribbons at supermarkets. Go into a Welsh mine with a hard hat. Now, that's a wonderful photo opportunity!"

She continued: "You could date former porn stars, you know—common women with a past. Get yourself photographed by *Paris Match* at all the wrong parties. Have a glamorous accident—you can use my helicopter!"

*T*he Prince was puzzled but promised his mother he would try
to be more royal. The Queen sighed in relief.

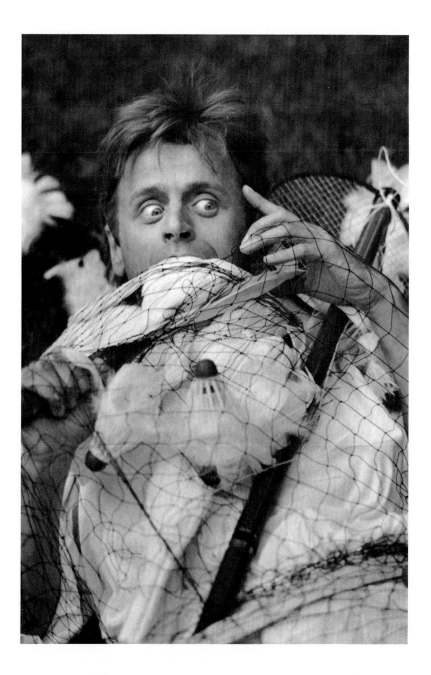

$\mathcal{H}$e tried badminton, a very genteel game . . .

. . . *mais non,* he was no John McEnroe.

*H*e took up horses,
the sport of kings . . .

. . . but took second place in the Swanee Downs.

His mother was not impressed. She had to try a new tack. She sent him to the renowned sex therapist Doctor Trudeliese Weisenheimer, who diagnosed acute ornithologico-sclerosis, commonly known as the Tchaikovsky Syndrome.

But the Prince became suspicious of her notes.

$\mathcal{A}$nd the young man's fantasy turned to . . .

. . . thoughts of revenge.

He was sent to Slimy-Schloss,
the German spa,
to take the waters.
But he only wanted to sing
Lohengrin in the tub.

Not even Frau Diesel, the Berlin foot-fetishist, could cure him.

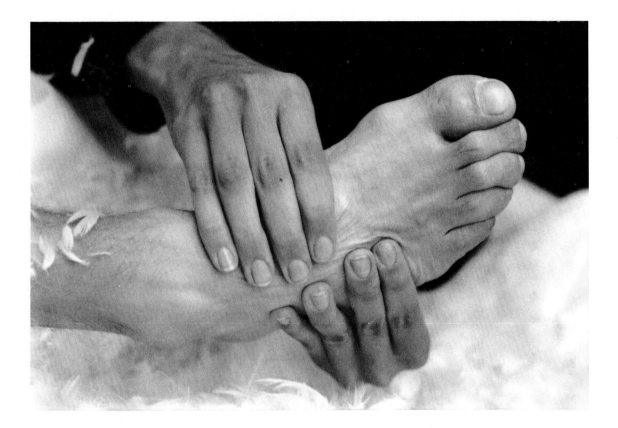

Kyrie eleison . . .

In desperation, his mother bade him seek salvation through the Church.

Surely, she thought, The Metropolitan Neurotikoff could exorcise the feathered demons from Siegfried's heart.

Prayers were offered . . .

candles lit . . .

incense burned . . .

and burned . . .

and burned . . .

. . . and smoldered

. . . and died.

*B*ut Siegfried felt like a Swan-Martyr.

The Queen began to fear that her son's case might be hopeless. But she held on to the dream that by some miracle the Prince might someday become a *real man* — a Bogart, a Brando, a Belmondo . . . a Danny Aiello.

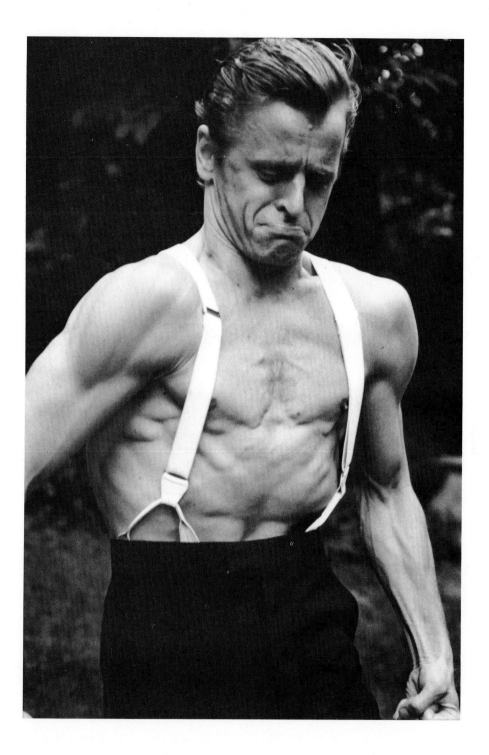

*H*aving exposed her son to women, sports, psychiatry, mineral baths, foot massage, and the Orthodox Church, all to no avail, the Queen took matters into her own beautifully manicured hands. She gave a dinner party!

She surrounded the Prince with all the most eligible Princesses in the land and had the affair catered by Le Gastronome.

$\mathcal{B}$ut Siegfried rejected these beauties one by one. They just weren't right. There was something missing. A certain *je ne sais quoi*. They didn't have . . . well . . . uh . . . any . . . feathers!

*S*urprise! To everyone's amazement, who should appear at the fête but

the elegant magician Von Rothbart. He enticed the Prince with some of his most glamorous creations.

$\mathscr{A}$las, the Prince abandoned the celebrations.

"Will I ever be happy?" he mused. "Will I ever meet a swan I can take home to Mother?"

And just then, sweet and strange music wafted across the water. . . .

$\mathcal{A}$nd suddenly there she was.

*T*hose eyes . . . those lips . . . that beak.

And they both danced happily ever after.

SPECIAL THANKS TO

Charles Engell France

AND ESPECIALLY TO

Jean Poniatowski
Les Éditions Condé Nast
Paris Vogue

PHOTOGRAPHIC PRINTS BY

Ronit Avneri

Many thanks to

Jack Ader
Azzedine Alaïa
American Ballet Theatre
Julie Ander
Ariane
Robin Atlas
Bonnie Berman
Beth Ann Management
Jim Brusock
Cerruti
Anne-Marie Chalmeton de Croÿ
Cecilia Chancellor
Christiaan
Click Model Management, Inc.
Enrico Coveri
Francine Crescent
Jean-Rémy Daumas
Oscar de la Renta
Christian Dior
Anthony Elgort
Elite Model Management, Inc.
Larisa Fielding
Ford Models, Inc.
A. Richard Golub
Gabrielle Grotewold
Wendy Harned
Iman
Jocelyn Kargère
Orlando King
Carole Kismaric
Karl Lagerfeld
Lanvin
Guy Laroche

Marianne
Charlie Marouani
Kristen McMenamy
The Metropolitan Opera
Julia Morton
Thierry Mugler
Name Model Management, Inc.
Philip Newton
New York City Ballet
Christopher Nofziger
Paulina
Florence Pettan
Mimi Potworowska
Montgomery Preston
Fabien Ranaivo
Susan Raney
Richard Reed
Karolla Ritter
Sonia Rykiel
Yves Saint Laurent
Morten Sandtroen
Mary Shanahan
Uma Thurman
Isabelle Townsend
Christy Turlington
Ungaro
Valentino
Gianni Versace
Village Eye, Opticians
Edgar Vincent
Paul Wagner
Laura Zarubin